THIS PLAN BOOK BELONGS TO:

_____

GRADE LEVEL: _____

SCHOOL YEAR: _____

WEEK AT A *Glance*

	MONDAY	TUESDAY	WEDNESDAY	THURSDAY	FRIDAY
GROUP:					
GROUP:					
GROUP:					
GROUP:					
GROUP:					

WEEK AT A *Glance*

	MONDAY	TUESDAY	WEDNESDAY	THURSDAY	FRIDAY
GROUP:					
GROUP:					
GROUP:					
GROUP:					
GROUP:					

WEEK AT A *Glance*

	MONDAY	TUESDAY	WEDNESDAY	THURSDAY	FRIDAY
GROUP:					
GROUP:					
GROUP:					
GROUP:					
GROUP:					

WEEK AT A *Glance*

	MONDAY	TUESDAY	WEDNESDAY	THURSDAY	FRIDAY
GROUP:					
GROUP:					
GROUP:					
GROUP:					
GROUP:					

WEEK AT A *Glance*

	MONDAY	TUESDAY	WEDNESDAY	THURSDAY	FRIDAY
GROUP:					
GROUP:					
GROUP:					
GROUP:					
GROUP:					

WEEK AT A *Glance*

	MONDAY	TUESDAY	WEDNESDAY	THURSDAY	FRIDAY
GROUP:					
GROUP:					
GROUP:					
GROUP:					
GROUP:					

WEEK AT A *Glance*

	MONDAY	TUESDAY	WEDNESDAY	THURSDAY	FRIDAY
GROUP:					
GROUP:					
GROUP:					
GROUP:					
GROUP:					

WEEK AT A *Glance*

	MONDAY	TUESDAY	WEDNESDAY	THURSDAY	FRIDAY
GROUP:					
GROUP:					
GROUP:					
GROUP:					
GROUP:					

WEEK AT A *Glance*

	MONDAY	TUESDAY	WEDNESDAY	THURSDAY	FRIDAY
GROUP:					
GROUP:					
GROUP:					
GROUP:					
GROUP:					

WEEK AT A *Glance*

	MONDAY	TUESDAY	WEDNESDAY	THURSDAY	FRIDAY
GROUP:					
GROUP:					
GROUP:					
GROUP:					
GROUP:					

WEEK AT A *Glance*

	MONDAY	TUESDAY	WEDNESDAY	THURSDAY	FRIDAY
GROUP:					
GROUP:					
GROUP:					
GROUP:					
GROUP:					

WEEK AT A *Glance*

	MONDAY	TUESDAY	WEDNESDAY	THURSDAY	FRIDAY
GROUP:					
GROUP:					
GROUP:					
GROUP:					
GROUP:					

WEEK AT A *Glance*

	MONDAY	TUESDAY	WEDNESDAY	THURSDAY	FRIDAY
GROUP:					
GROUP:					
GROUP:					
GROUP:					
GROUP:					

WEEK AT A *Glance*

	MONDAY	TUESDAY	WEDNESDAY	THURSDAY	FRIDAY
GROUP:					
GROUP:					
GROUP:					
GROUP:					
GROUP:					

WEEK AT A *Glance*

	MONDAY	TUESDAY	WEDNESDAY	THURSDAY	FRIDAY
GROUP:					
GROUP:					
GROUP:					
GROUP:					
GROUP:					

WEEK AT A *Glance*

	MONDAY	TUESDAY	WEDNESDAY	THURSDAY	FRIDAY
GROUP:					
GROUP:					
GROUP:					
GROUP:					
GROUP:					

WEEK AT A *Glance*

	MONDAY	TUESDAY	WEDNESDAY	THURSDAY	FRIDAY
GROUP:					
GROUP:					
GROUP:					
GROUP:					
GROUP:					

LESSON *Plan*

GROUP:	DATE:
BOOK TITLE:	LEVEL:

TEACHING POINT / STRATEGY

WORD WORK	VOCABULARY

BEFORE READING

DURING READING

AFTER READING

NOTES

ANECDOTAL Notes

STUDENT NAME	OBSERVATIONS	NOTES

LESSON *Plan*

GROUP:	DATE:
BOOK TITLE:	LEVEL:

TEACHING POINT / STRATEGY

WORD WORK	VOCABULARY

BEFORE READING

DURING READING

AFTER READING

NOTES

ANECDOTAL *Notes*

STUDENT NAME	OBSERVATIONS	NOTES

LESSON Plan

GROUP: DATE:

BOOK TITLE: LEVEL:

TEACHING POINT / STRATEGY

WORD WORK	VOCABULARY

BEFORE READING

DURING READING

AFTER READING

NOTES

ANECDOTAL Notes

STUDENT NAME	OBSERVATIONS	NOTES

LESSON *Plan*

GROUP:	DATE:
BOOK TITLE:	LEVEL:

TEACHING POINT / STRATEGY

WORD WORK	VOCABULARY

BEFORE READING

DURING READING

AFTER READING

NOTES

ANECDOTAL Notes

STUDENT NAME	OBSERVATIONS	NOTES

LESSON Plan

GROUP: DATE:

BOOK TITLE: LEVEL:

TEACHING POINT / STRATEGY	
WORD WORK	VOCABULARY

BEFORE READING

DURING READING

AFTER READING

NOTES

ANECDOTAL *Notes*

STUDENT NAME	OBSERVATIONS	NOTES

LESSON *Plan*

GROUP:	DATE:
BOOK TITLE:	LEVEL:

TEACHING POINT / STRATEGY

WORD WORK	VOCABULARY

BEFORE READING

DURING READING

AFTER READING

NOTES

ANECDOTAL Notes

STUDENT NAME	OBSERVATIONS	NOTES

LESSON *Plan*

GROUP: DATE:

BOOK TITLE: LEVEL:

TEACHING POINT / STRATEGY

WORD WORK	VOCABULARY

BEFORE READING

DURING READING

AFTER READING

NOTES

ANECDOTAL Notes

STUDENT NAME	OBSERVATIONS	NOTES

LESSON *Plan*

GROUP: DATE:

BOOK TITLE: LEVEL:

TEACHING POINT / STRATEGY

WORD WORK	VOCABULARY

BEFORE READING

DURING READING

AFTER READING

NOTES

ANECDOTAL Notes

STUDENT NAME	OBSERVATIONS	NOTES

LESSON *Plan*

GROUP:	DATE:
BOOK TITLE:	LEVEL:

TEACHING POINT / STRATEGY

WORD WORK	VOCABULARY

BEFORE READING

DURING READING

AFTER READING

NOTES

ANECDOTAL Notes

STUDENT NAME	OBSERVATIONS	NOTES

LESSON Plan

GROUP:	DATE:
BOOK TITLE:	LEVEL:

TEACHING POINT / STRATEGY

WORD WORK	VOCABULARY

BEFORE READING

DURING READING

AFTER READING

NOTES

ANECDOTAL *Notes*

STUDENT NAME	OBSERVATIONS	NOTES

LESSON *Plan*

GROUP: DATE:

BOOK TITLE: LEVEL:

TEACHING POINT / STRATEGY

WORD WORK	VOCABULARY

BEFORE READING

DURING READING

AFTER READING

NOTES

ANECDOTAL *Notes*

STUDENT NAME	OBSERVATIONS	NOTES

LESSON *Plan*

GROUP: DATE:

BOOK TITLE: LEVEL:

TEACHING POINT / STRATEGY

WORD WORK	VOCABULARY

BEFORE READING

DURING READING

AFTER READING

NOTES

ANECDOTAL Notes

STUDENT NAME	OBSERVATIONS	NOTES

LESSON *Plan*

GROUP: DATE:

BOOK TITLE: LEVEL:

TEACHING POINT / STRATEGY

WORD WORK	VOCABULARY

BEFORE READING

DURING READING

AFTER READING

NOTES

ANECDOTAL Notes

STUDENT NAME	OBSERVATIONS	NOTES

LESSON *Plan*

GROUP: DATE:

BOOK TITLE: LEVEL:

TEACHING POINT / STRATEGY

WORD WORK	VOCABULARY

BEFORE READING

DURING READING

AFTER READING

NOTES

ANECDOTAL *Notes*

STUDENT NAME	OBSERVATIONS	NOTES

LESSON *Plan*

GROUP: DATE:

BOOK TITLE: LEVEL:

TEACHING POINT / STRATEGY

WORD WORK	VOCABULARY

BEFORE READING

DURING READING

AFTER READING

NOTES

ANECDOTAL *Notes*

STUDENT NAME	OBSERVATIONS	NOTES

LESSON *Plan*

GROUP: DATE:

BOOK TITLE: LEVEL:

TEACHING POINT / STRATEGY

WORD WORK	VOCABULARY

BEFORE READING

DURING READING

AFTER READING

NOTES

ANECDOTAL Notes

STUDENT NAME	OBSERVATIONS	NOTES

LESSON *Plan*

GROUP:	DATE:
BOOK TITLE:	LEVEL:

TEACHING POINT / STRATEGY

WORD WORK	VOCABULARY

BEFORE READING

DURING READING

AFTER READING

NOTES

ANECDOTAL *Notes*

STUDENT NAME	OBSERVATIONS	NOTES

LESSON *Plan*

GROUP:	DATE:
BOOK TITLE:	LEVEL:

TEACHING POINT / STRATEGY

WORD WORK	VOCABULARY

BEFORE READING

DURING READING

AFTER READING

NOTES

ANECDOTAL Notes

STUDENT NAME	OBSERVATIONS	NOTES

LESSON *Plan*

GROUP: DATE:

BOOK TITLE: LEVEL:

TEACHING POINT / STRATEGY

WORD WORK	VOCABULARY

BEFORE READING

DURING READING

AFTER READING

NOTES

ANECDOTAL *Notes*

STUDENT NAME	OBSERVATIONS	NOTES

LESSON *Plan*

GROUP:	DATE:
BOOK TITLE:	LEVEL:

TEACHING POINT / STRATEGY

WORD WORK	VOCABULARY

BEFORE READING

DURING READING

AFTER READING

NOTES

ANECDOTAL *Notes*

STUDENT NAME	OBSERVATIONS	NOTES

LESSON *Plan*

GROUP:	DATE:
BOOK TITLE:	LEVEL:

TEACHING POINT / STRATEGY

WORD WORK	VOCABULARY

BEFORE READING

DURING READING

AFTER READING

NOTES

ANECDOTAL *Notes*

STUDENT NAME	OBSERVATIONS	NOTES

LESSON *Plan*

GROUP:	DATE:
BOOK TITLE:	LEVEL:

TEACHING POINT / STRATEGY

WORD WORK	VOCABULARY

BEFORE READING

DURING READING

AFTER READING

NOTES

ANECDOTAL Notes

STUDENT NAME	OBSERVATIONS	NOTES

LESSON *Plan*

GROUP: DATE:

BOOK TITLE: LEVEL:

TEACHING POINT / STRATEGY

WORD WORK	VOCABULARY

BEFORE READING

DURING READING

AFTER READING

NOTES

ANECDOTAL *Notes*

STUDENT NAME	OBSERVATIONS	NOTES

LESSON *Plan*

GROUP:	DATE:
BOOK TITLE:	LEVEL:

TEACHING POINT / STRATEGY

WORD WORK	VOCABULARY

BEFORE READING

DURING READING

AFTER READING

NOTES

ANECDOTAL *Notes*

STUDENT NAME	OBSERVATIONS	NOTES

LESSON *Plan*

GROUP: DATE:

BOOK TITLE: LEVEL:

TEACHING POINT / STRATEGY

WORD WORK	VOCABULARY

BEFORE READING

DURING READING

AFTER READING

NOTES

ANECDOTAL Notes

STUDENT NAME	OBSERVATIONS	NOTES

LESSON *Plan*

GROUP: DATE:

BOOK TITLE: LEVEL:

TEACHING POINT / STRATEGY

WORD WORK	VOCABULARY

BEFORE READING

DURING READING

AFTER READING

NOTES

ANECDOTAL Notes

STUDENT NAME	OBSERVATIONS	NOTES

LESSON Plan

GROUP: DATE:

BOOK TITLE: LEVEL:

TEACHING POINT / STRATEGY

WORD WORK	VOCABULARY

BEFORE READING

DURING READING

AFTER READING

NOTES

ANECDOTAL *Notes*

STUDENT NAME	OBSERVATIONS	NOTES

LESSON *Plan*

GROUP: DATE:

BOOK TITLE: LEVEL:

TEACHING POINT / STRATEGY

WORD WORK	VOCABULARY

BEFORE READING

DURING READING

AFTER READING

NOTES

ANECDOTAL *Notes*

STUDENT NAME	OBSERVATIONS	NOTES

LESSON *Plan*

GROUP: DATE:

BOOK TITLE: LEVEL:

TEACHING POINT / STRATEGY

WORD WORK	VOCABULARY

BEFORE READING

DURING READING

AFTER READING

NOTES

ANECDOTAL Notes

STUDENT NAME	OBSERVATIONS	NOTES

LESSON *Plan*

GROUP:	DATE:
BOOK TITLE:	LEVEL:

TEACHING POINT / STRATEGY

WORD WORK	VOCABULARY

BEFORE READING

DURING READING

AFTER READING

NOTES

ANECDOTAL *Notes*

STUDENT NAME	OBSERVATIONS	NOTES

LESSON *Plan*

GROUP: DATE:

BOOK TITLE: LEVEL:

TEACHING POINT / STRATEGY

WORD WORK	VOCABULARY

BEFORE READING

DURING READING

AFTER READING

NOTES

ANECDOTAL Notes

STUDENT NAME	OBSERVATIONS	NOTES

LESSON Plan

GROUP: DATE:

BOOK TITLE: LEVEL:

TEACHING POINT / STRATEGY

WORD WORK	VOCABULARY

BEFORE READING

DURING READING

AFTER READING

NOTES

ANECDOTAL *Notes*

STUDENT NAME	OBSERVATIONS	NOTES

LESSON *Plan*

GROUP: DATE:

BOOK TITLE: LEVEL:

TEACHING POINT / STRATEGY

WORD WORK	VOCABULARY

BEFORE READING

DURING READING

AFTER READING

NOTES

ANECDOTAL Notes

STUDENT NAME	OBSERVATIONS	NOTES

LESSON Plan

GROUP: DATE:

BOOK TITLE: LEVEL:

TEACHING POINT / STRATEGY	
WORD WORK	VOCABULARY

BEFORE READING

DURING READING

AFTER READING

NOTES

ANECDOTAL *Notes*

STUDENT NAME	OBSERVATIONS	NOTES

LESSON Plan

GROUP: DATE:

BOOK TITLE: LEVEL:

TEACHING POINT / STRATEGY

WORD WORK	VOCABULARY

BEFORE READING

DURING READING

AFTER READING

NOTES

ANECDOTAL *Notes*

STUDENT NAME	OBSERVATIONS	NOTES

LESSON *Plan*

GROUP:	DATE:
BOOK TITLE:	LEVEL:

TEACHING POINT / STRATEGY

WORD WORK	VOCABULARY

BEFORE READING

DURING READING

AFTER READING

NOTES

ANECDOTAL *Notes*

STUDENT NAME	OBSERVATIONS	NOTES

LESSON *Plan*

GROUP: DATE:

BOOK TITLE: LEVEL:

TEACHING POINT / STRATEGY

WORD WORK	VOCABULARY

BEFORE READING

DURING READING

AFTER READING

NOTES

ANECDOTAL Notes

STUDENT NAME	OBSERVATIONS	NOTES

LESSON *Plan*

GROUP:	DATE:
BOOK TITLE:	LEVEL:

TEACHING POINT / STRATEGY

WORD WORK	VOCABULARY

BEFORE READING

DURING READING

AFTER READING

NOTES

ANECDOTAL *Notes*

STUDENT NAME	OBSERVATIONS	NOTES

LESSON *Plan*

GROUP:	DATE:
BOOK TITLE:	LEVEL:

TEACHING POINT / STRATEGY

WORD WORK	VOCABULARY

BEFORE READING

DURING READING

AFTER READING

NOTES

ANECDOTAL Notes

STUDENT NAME	OBSERVATIONS	NOTES

LESSON Plan

GROUP:	DATE:
BOOK TITLE:	LEVEL:

TEACHING POINT / STRATEGY

WORD WORK	VOCABULARY

BEFORE READING

DURING READING

AFTER READING

NOTES

ANECDOTAL *Notes*

STUDENT NAME	OBSERVATIONS	NOTES

LESSON *Plan*

GROUP: DATE:

BOOK TITLE: LEVEL:

TEACHING POINT / STRATEGY

WORD WORK	VOCABULARY

BEFORE READING

DURING READING

AFTER READING

NOTES

ANECDOTAL Notes

STUDENT NAME	OBSERVATIONS	NOTES

LESSON *Plan*

GROUP: DATE:

BOOK TITLE: LEVEL:

TEACHING POINT / STRATEGY

WORD WORK	VOCABULARY

BEFORE READING

DURING READING

AFTER READING

NOTES

ANECDOTAL *Notes*

STUDENT NAME	OBSERVATIONS	NOTES

LESSON *Plan*

GROUP:	DATE:
BOOK TITLE:	LEVEL:

TEACHING POINT / STRATEGY

WORD WORK	VOCABULARY

BEFORE READING

DURING READING

AFTER READING

NOTES

ANECDOTAL Notes

STUDENT NAME	OBSERVATIONS	NOTES

LESSON Plan

GROUP: DATE:

BOOK TITLE: LEVEL:

TEACHING POINT / STRATEGY

WORD WORK	VOCABULARY

BEFORE READING

DURING READING

AFTER READING

NOTES

ANECDOTAL Notes

STUDENT NAME	OBSERVATIONS	NOTES

LESSON Plan

GROUP: DATE:

BOOK TITLE: LEVEL:

TEACHING POINT / STRATEGY

WORD WORK	VOCABULARY

BEFORE READING

DURING READING

AFTER READING

NOTES

ANECDOTAL *Notes*

STUDENT NAME	OBSERVATIONS	NOTES

LESSON Plan

GROUP: DATE:

BOOK TITLE: LEVEL:

TEACHING POINT / STRATEGY

WORD WORK	VOCABULARY

BEFORE READING

DURING READING

AFTER READING

NOTES

ANECDOTAL *Notes*

STUDENT NAME	OBSERVATIONS	NOTES

LESSON Plan

GROUP: DATE:

BOOK TITLE: LEVEL:

TEACHING POINT / STRATEGY

WORD WORK	VOCABULARY

BEFORE READING

DURING READING

AFTER READING

NOTES

ANECDOTAL *Notes*

STUDENT NAME	OBSERVATIONS	NOTES

LESSON *Plan*

GROUP:	DATE:
BOOK TITLE:	LEVEL:

TEACHING POINT / STRATEGY

WORD WORK	VOCABULARY

BEFORE READING

DURING READING

AFTER READING

NOTES

ANECDOTAL *Notes*

STUDENT NAME	OBSERVATIONS	NOTES

LESSON *Plan*

GROUP:	DATE:
BOOK TITLE:	LEVEL:

TEACHING POINT / STRATEGY

WORD WORK	VOCABULARY

BEFORE READING

DURING READING

AFTER READING

NOTES

ANECDOTAL Notes

STUDENT NAME	OBSERVATIONS	NOTES

LESSON Plan

GROUP: DATE:

BOOK TITLE: LEVEL:

TEACHING POINT / STRATEGY

WORD WORK	VOCABULARY

BEFORE READING

DURING READING

AFTER READING

NOTES

ANECDOTAL Notes

STUDENT NAME	OBSERVATIONS	NOTES

Thank you!

For enquiries and feedback, please email us:

365teacherresources@gmail.com

Made in the USA
Monee, IL
05 March 2022

92313668R00070